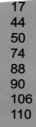

CONTENTS

Norfolk for Photographers
By Stephen Kelly
All Copyright © 2015 Kellys Guides
kellysguides@gmail.com
ISBN 978-0-9935536-0-8

Published in the United Kingdom
First edition, 2016

Kelly's Guides
Norwich
NR4 6AY
United Kingdom

Although the author and publisher have made
every effort to ensure that the information
in this book was correct, the author and
publisher do not assume and hereby disclaim
any liability to any party for any loss, damage,
or disruption caused by errors or omissions,
whether such errors or omissions result from
negligence, accident, or any other cause.

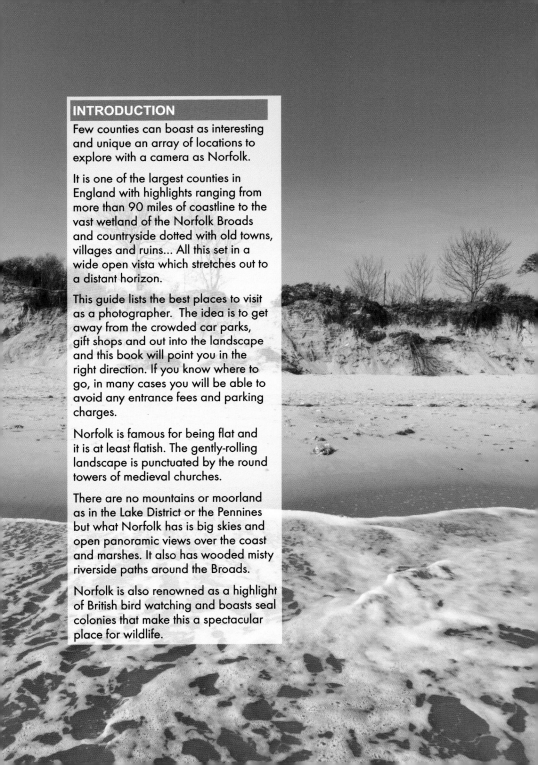

INTRODUCTION

Few counties can boast as interesting and unique an array of locations to explore with a camera as Norfolk.

It is one of the largest counties in England with highlights ranging from more than 90 miles of coastline to the vast wetland of the Norfolk Broads and countryside dotted with old towns, villages and ruins... All this set in a wide open vista which stretches out to a distant horizon.

This guide lists the best places to visit as a photographer. The idea is to get away from the crowded car parks, gift shops and out into the landscape and this book will point you in the right direction. If you know where to go, in many cases you will be able to avoid any entrance fees and parking charges.

Norfolk is famous for being flat and it is at least flatish. The gently-rolling landscape is punctuated by the round towers of medieval churches.

There are no mountains or moorland as in the Lake District or the Pennines but what Norfolk has is big skies and open panoramic views over the coast and marshes. It also has wooded misty riverside paths around the Broads.

Norfolk is also renowned as a highlight of British bird watching and boasts seal colonies that make this a spectacular place for wildlife.

There is also the historic city of Norwich with an abundance of picture opportunities. Affluent during the Middle Ages due to the wool trade, it was England's second city. The wealth can be seen in the buildings and ruins left behind.

But it's not just Norwich which has glories from the past; King's Lynn is home to what architectural historian Sir Nikolaus Pevsner described as "one of the most perfect buildings ever built"

Bordered on three sides by the sea, this has never been a place you pass through. There's not an inch of motorway and this isolation has helped to protect the county's charm.

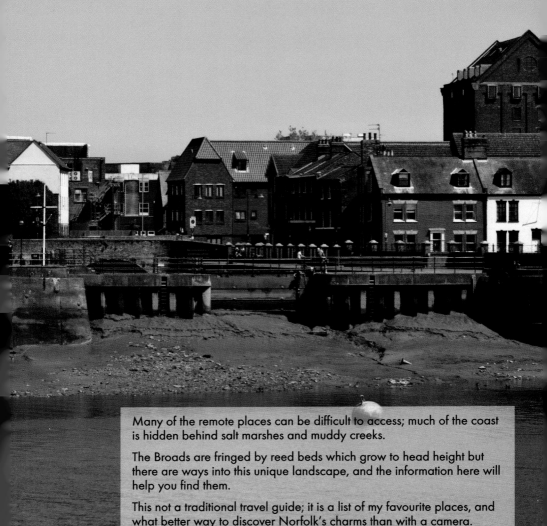

It is Norfolk's location that has helped protect it. The Industrial Revolution never really reached this far; for centuries the rest of the world forgot about it this corner of England.

Outside the medieval city of Norwich there was little urban sprawl and it is this absence of development that makes Norfolk so special and attractive to outsiders.

In recent years, however, tourists and incomers have rediscovered the unspoilt beauty of the Broads and the long coastline and Norfolk is affluent once more with holidaymakers and second-home owners pouring money into parts of the county.

Many of the remote places can be difficult to access; much of the coast is hidden behind salt marshes and muddy creeks.

The Broads are fringed by reed beds which grow to head height but there are ways into this unique landscape, and the information here will help you find them.

This not a traditional travel guide; it is a list of my favourite places, and what better way to discover Norfolk's charms than with a camera.

NORFOLK

© Kelly's guides

WILDLIFE

BUILDINGS AND RUINS

COAST RIVERS AND BROADS

3

WEST NORFOLK AND KING'S LYNN

The Fens stretch over three counties and this is where Norfolk gets its reputation for being flat. It is, but it's anything but featureless.

This manmade landscape has been drained by successive generations, creating hugely fertile agricultural land which made the locals very rich, and they spent their wealth on their splendid churches.

King's Lynn is the capital of this part of The Fens. The town was one of the major ports of medieval England. As a member of the Hanseatic League the towns trading influence spread across the North Sea. Much of the historic splendour survives in the old town.

King's Lynn lies at one corner of the square shaped bay and estuary of The Wash. This is one of the most important wetland habitats in Europe, and a mecca for birdwatchers.

DON'T MISS

The Custom House
Wiggenhall St Marys
The River Great Ouse
Red Mount Chapel
Sandringham Estate

1. WEST LYNN

The Great Ouse is one of the main channels draining the Fens into The Wash. West Lynn on the western bank has good views of historic King's Lynn waterfront. A foot passenger ferry links the two halves of King's Lynn.

PE34 3JQ on street parking

2. KING'S LYNN OLD TOWN

Medieval King's Lynn was one of the major ports of England. As a member of the Hanseatic League the towns trading influence spread across the North Sea to the Baltic. Much of the historic splendour survives around Queen Street and the Minster church.

The gold coloured stonework glows in evening setting sunlight.

PE30 5DL pay and display or park on South Quay

WEST NORFOLK

3

3. KING'S LYNN SOUTH QUAY

The river front has colourful fishing boats and redeveloped warehouses. The beautifully proportioned Custom House overlooks the old port area. Architectural historian Nikolaus Pevsner described it as "one of the most perfect buildings ever built".
PE30 5DT on street parking

4. RED MOUNT CHAPEL

This strange building was built in 1485 and was used by pilgrims on their way to Walsingham. The chapel now sits on a mound in the town's park.
PE30 5EW on street parking

4

5. FISHER FLEET

Amongst an industrial landscape, Fisher Fleet is home to King's Lynn's fishing trade. Boats old and new line the creek. The skeletons of wooden hulls and landing stages rot in the mud.
PE30 2ET

6. WIGGENHALL

Wiggenhall is a collection of villages named after saints and its monastic wealth can be seen in its churches. The Carved pews in St Mary's are amongst the best in England. The drainage channels criss-cross the landscape. The River Great Ouse is the oldest with a footpath on both banks, making a nice walk between the villages.
St Mary's PE34 3EJ
Great Ouse PE34 3EU

7. CASTLE RISING

A 12th Century castle, the stone keep is one of the best of its kind in England and sits in the middle of high earthwork defences.
PE31 6AH admission charges

© Kelly's guides

9. DERSINGHAM BOG

A nature reserve on the edge of the Sandringham Estate comprising bog heath and woodland.
PE35 6EJ free car park

8. SANDRINGHAM ESTATE

The Queen's huge country estate stretches from the house, out to The Wash. There is a visitors' centre and woodland to explore. Photographers with long lenses are discouraged when the Royals are in residence.
PE35 6EH free parking at visitors' centre

THE COAST

Much of Norfolk is dominated by its stunning coastline. The county is surrounded by remote and unspoiled beaches, marshes and cliffs.

The ravages of the North Sea's tides and storms regularly reshape the shore. Varied and imposing, it's a beautiful location for the landscape photographer.

The North Norfolk coast is unblemished by its popularity, its sheer scale still makes it easy to find empty epic panoramas.

It's not just the big vistas that the Norfolk coast has to offer, crumbling sea defences, long abandoned wrecks, all offer interesting subject to explore with a camera.

Miles of deserted beaches and creeks, backed by sand dunes and salt marshes, a place which lends itself to epic views, and as the weather changes spectacular cloudscapes and sunsets.

DON'T MISS

Holkham and Wells beach
Cromer and the Pier
Hunstantons stripped cliffs
Brancater staithe
Wintherton seal colony

10. SNETTISHAM

This nature reserve overlooks the estuary of The Wash. The ramshackle collection of seaside caravans and shacks shouldn't put you off. The spectacle is out to sea. As the tide starts to come in, huge numbers of wading birds are pushed up the mud banks, creating swirling patterns as the flocks keep ahead of the advancing tide.

PE31 7PS car park charges

11. BAWSEY CHURCH

The ruins of a small church stand on raised ground overlooking farmland, like a miniature Glastonbury Tor.

PE32 1EU rough farm track off the B1145 signpost for Church Farm

12. HUNSTANTON CLIFFS

The cliffs on the northern edge of the seaside town alternate with red and white bands. At low tide there is the iron backbone and ribs of an old shipwreck to use as a good foreground. Also at low tide, green seaweed-covered pillows of rock line up in rows at the water's edge. Because it faces east it is one of the only places on the whole of this side of the country where the sun sets over the sea.

PE36 6HJ on street parking above cliffs

13. BRANCASTER BEACH

A wide open beach which stretches until the land meets the sky. A good place to capture Norfolk's Big Skies. The distant horizon shimmering is perfect for landscapes and sunsets and also popular with acrobatic kite surfers.
PE31 8AX pay and display

14. BRANCASTER STAITHE

Amongst the marshes, this small working fishing harbour has colourful working boats, lobster pots and a traditional polished wooden sailing fleet. The muddy creeks and marshes along the coastal path are also good to explore.
PE31 8BW or walk down from Barrow Common

15. BARROW COMMON

This heath land on high ground has great panoramic views along the North Norfolk coastline.

PE31 8DB parking in lay-bys

16. GUN HILL BEACH

It's a two mile walk from the road to these remote sand dunes overlooking the beach and creeks. Across the main channel is Scolt Head Island, made up of shingle and sand dunes, created by deposits from erosion further along the coast. This is another Big Skies location. The tide can be dangerous along this stretch of coast, so make sure you start any walk as the tide is going out and always have a route planned for when the tide turns.

PE31 8JJ small parking at T junction with footpath opposite

Norfolk for photographers

17. BURNHAM MARKET

A village nicknamed "Chelsea-on-Sea" because of the takeover by London weekenders, choked by expensive 4x4s, best avoided.

18. BURNHAM OVERY

The village and staithe of Burnham Overy still retains the character and atmosphere which has been lost from its trendy neighbour Burnham Market. Paths and lanes lead from the church to the staithe. The churchyard has some interesting gravestones.

PE31 8HX Church
PE31 8JF staithe

THE COAST

22

19. HOLKHAM BEACH

Beach and sand dunes fringed by pine forests, made famous as the location for the final scene of Shakespeare in Love. There is a good circular walk via town then back through the park of Holkham house.

NR23 1RG park in village

20. HOLKHAM ESTATE

A typical village of a large country estate, picturesque cottages line the drive to the Hall. The house itself sits in the middle of beautiful parkland with a lake and deer herd.

NR23 1RG Park in village

21. WELLS BEACH

A line of colourful beach huts stretch along the edge of the dunes and pine woods. Built on legs above the shifting sands, these sheds on legs are sought after by London weekenders and can change hands for £60,000. NR23 1DR expensive beach car park. Alternatively walk from town or catch miniature train along beach road.

22. WELLS-NEXT-THE-SEA

This is the biggest harbour between King's Lynn and Great Yarmouth. Wells is one mile up a creek from the sea. There are often colourful fishing boats and old sailing ships tied up at the quay with old warehouses behind. A good vantage point is along the coast path to the east looking back at the town along the creek and over the marshes. NR23 1EX on street parking around the Buttlands green.

23. MORSTON QUAY

One of the many inlets used as sheltered mooring and the starting point for boat trips out to Blakeney Point seal colony, many wooden landing stages and rotting hulls line the creeks. It is even more atmospheric when the mist comes down. NR25 7BL NT car park or limited free parking by church

24. BLAKENEY POINT SEALS

This is one of the must see wildlife spectacles in England, a thriving colony of common and grey seals live on this isolated spit of land. Boat trips leave from Morston Quay out to the point. The boats sail close to the sand banks, inquisitive seals often swimming alongside.

You can explore the point on foot, but it's not encouraged to approach the seals on land.

NR25 7BL boats leave from Morston Quay. Times and tickets sold in the village.

28

25. BLAKENEY

This is another of the pretty North Norfolk villages with good walks along the coast path and out over the marshes. Access to the beach is cut off by creeks.

NR25 7ND NT car park

26. CLEY BEACH

This is the landward end of Blakeney Point.

A stark beautiful shingle bank with marshes behind, very popular with birdwatchers, because it can be the first landfall for many migrant species. Some of the shapes of the shingle and old sea defences are almost sculptural and abstract.

NR25 7RZ car park by beach or lay-bys on coast road between Cley and Salthouse

27. CLEY MILL

The windmill at Cley stands tall over the marsh, giving a sense of scale to the surrounding landscape.
NR25 7RP limited on street parking

28. BARD HILL, SALTHOUSE

High ground overlooking the marshes and coast with Salthouse church in the foreground. It's a beautiful walk down through the village and along the beach.
NR25 7XD parking along tracks on heath

29. WEYBOURNE STATION

This is a station and engine sheds for the North Norfolk steam railway. Paths lead in both directions following the line of the tracks, towards Sheringham Park to the east and Kelling Heath to the west.

NR25 7HN limited parking

30. WEYBOURNE

All along the North Norfolk coast old tractors are used to pull fishing boats up the shingle beaches. At Weybourne there are some interesting and typical examples. Corroded by the salted water, it looks like these old machines are rusted to the spot.

NR25 7SR parking charges or walk along the coast path from Sheringham or Salthouse

34. BEESTON BUMP

This is one of the most prominent and highest points along the Norfolk coast, with views over the town of Sheringham.

NR26 8BL on street parking around town

31. SHERINGHAM PARK

A National Trust estate with park land designed by Humphry Repton, the house nestles in a valley overlooked by a Grecian folly. The drive is lined with rhododendrons. Around the park, viewing platforms have been built above the treetops, giving spectacular views.

NR26 8TL NT car park or walk from Weybourne

32. HOLT

A pleasant market town, which has had much of the character, drained out of it by weekenders and up market gift shops.

33. SHERINGHAM

A small town built overlooking a shingle beach, colourful fishing boats are winched up on two slipways.

NR26 8BW paking as for Beeston

THE COAST

Norfolk for photographers

35. CROMER

This is arguably the best seaside town in Norfolk, with sandy beaches and pier. A fishing fleet sails from the beach to catch the famous Cromer crabs. East from the town there is a fantastic cliff top walk to the next village of Overstrand. Time it right, so the tide is out for a walk back along the beach. Look out for spectacular sunsets reflected on the wet sand as the waves recede. Hunt for hag stones amongst the pebbles; pieces of flint with natural holes once prized as fishing weights.
NR27 9EF pay and display car park or on street parking, or
NR27 0PP walk from
Overstrand
pay and display car park or on street parking

THE COAST

36. HAPPISBURGH

This seaside village is slowly being washed into the sea. The mud cliffs are carved into interesting shapes as they are eroded by the action of waves and tide, overlooked by a famous red and white lighthouse.

NR12 0PR pay and display car park

37. WINTERTON SEALS

This is a stretch of unspoilt beach
and dunes, with a large seal
colony 1 mile to the north, a
fantastic wildlife spectacle during
the winter breeding season.
NR29 4DD car park at beach or
on street in the village

38. BACONSTHORPE CASTLE

An atmospheric fortified 15th century manor house ruin, surrounded by a moat still full of water, which provides interesting foreground reflections.
NR25 6LB free parking at castle along farm track

39. LITTLE SNORING CHURCH

A typical charming round tower flint church, this is the finest in the county and has been the subject of many famous paintings
NR21 0HZ car park beside church

38

40. GREAT YARMOUTH

Yarmouth is Norfolk's largest seaside town and a world away from the genteel North Norfolk coast.

The wide sandy beach is backed by the lights of amusement arcades. The town was once a wealthy port, and many imposing Victorian buildings can be found around the Wellington Road area.
Great Yarmouth is well past its heyday and is now one of the poorest boroughs in England.

To the south amongst warehouses and factories is the first Nelson's column, built by the town to commemorate Norfolk's most famous son.

The town is built on a sand spit. The port and harbour were once the southern home to the British herring fleet. It's now used by support ships for the offshore gas and wind farm industry.
NR30 3JD Wellington Road and seafront
NR30 3PS Nelson's Monument
NR30 2RL South Quay port area

41. GORLESTON

At the mouth of Yarmouth harbour, Gorleston is the best place to watch the comings and goings from the busy port.

NR31 6PL on street parking

CASTLES, CHURCHES AND RUINS

A good ruin can make any landscape photograph, and Norfolk has some great ruins.

Because Norfolk's heyday was three centuries ago, during the medieval period, many ruined churches and castles were left in the landscape as villages have shrunk or been abandoned. These centuries of decline and isolation, have left behind a rich legacy to explore.

Norfolk's long history has left it rich in castles churches and ruins. The architectural history of the county stretches from the Roman occupation to Modernism.

Outside of Hadrian's Wall, not much remains of the Roman occupation of Britain.

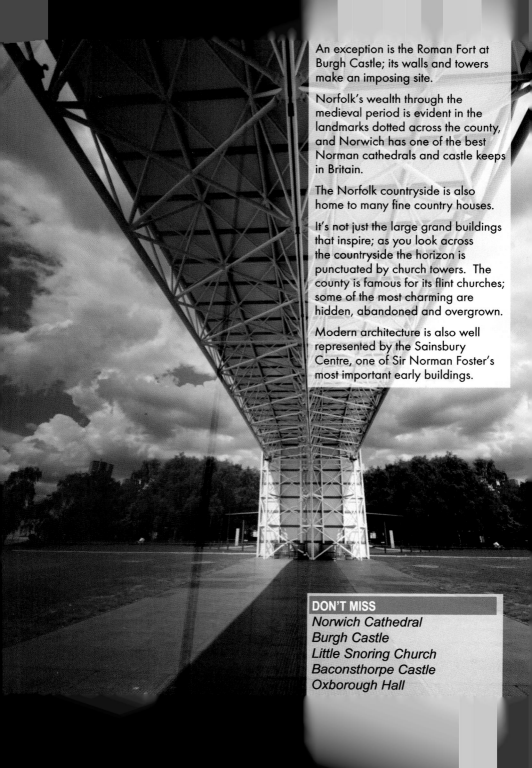

An exception is the Roman Fort at Burgh Castle; its walls and towers make an imposing site.

Norfolk's wealth through the medieval period is evident in the landmarks dotted across the county, and Norwich has one of the best Norman cathedrals and castle keeps in Britain.

The Norfolk countryside is also home to many fine country houses.

It's not just the large grand buildings that inspire; as you look across the countryside the horizon is punctuated by church towers. The county is famous for its flint churches; some of the most charming are hidden, abandoned and overgrown.

Modern architecture is also well represented by the Sainsbury Centre, one of Sir Norman Foster's most important early buildings.

DON'T MISS
Norwich Cathedral
Burgh Castle
Little Snoring Church
Baconsthorpe Castle
Oxborough Hall

42

42. BURGH CASTLE

This is one of the most impressive sites from the Roman period, second only to Hadrian's Wall. Three sides of the rectangular fort survive with flint and brick walls and round towers. The location is special because the fort was built to overlook and defend Breydon water, the entrance to The Broads.

Also worth exploring are the riverbank walks below the fort. The marshes stretch for miles inland. Amongst the reeds, half way across the marsh, is the Berney Arms which can only be accessed by train or the river.
NR31 9QB Free car park

42

43. BURGH ST PETER

An Interesting church with a tower made up of brick cubes, like child's building blocks. The staithe is also a good place to see the River Waveney which is the southern arm of the Broad's network.

NR34 0DD

44. THRIGBY ZOO

This is a small zoo with high walkways built above many of the enclosures, which give views down onto the animals, without having to look through the bars of a cage. It's also worth following the keepers round during feeding time.

NR29 3DR admission charges

45. BUCKENHAM ROOKERY

Huge flock of rooks and jackdaws fly into the woodland around Buckenham Church. They fly in to roost at dusk making them difficult to photograph, but they can be spectacular when shot against a sunset.

NR13 4HW free parking at station then walk back up lane to look towards church

46. HETHEL OLD THORN

This is claimed to be the smallest nature reserve in the UK. It consists of only one ancient hawthorn bush. Like at Glastonbury, local folk lore says the tree grew from the staff of Joseph of Arimathea.

NR14 8HE parking at the church the thorn is in the field behind

47.CANTLEY SUGAR FACTORY

An unusual location in the Broads, this busy factory can be seen from miles around. It's interesting to walk along the river and around the perimeter of this industrial landscape.

NR13 3SH Cantley staithe off Station Road

THE BROADS

The Norfolk Broads is made up of a network of rivers and lakes. The landscape can vary from shaded woodland in the west to wide expanses of marsh in the east. To the casual visitor, the broads can seem inaccessible; access to the water is often restricted by private land or a large expanse of reed beds.

If you know where to look, this is a unique landscape to explore.

The Broads are a busy tourist destination, popular for boating holidays. But there are many stretches of river which feel very remote; you can walk for miles across water meadows, marsh and along river banks without seeing a road let alone a house or person. The access to the river bank might be limited, but with the information of where to look, the Norfolk Broads opens up before you.
Much of this landscape is manmade; The Broads are old peat diggings; the fields drained by a network of windmills, properly called drainage pumps. Many now in ruins, they are scattered along the river banks, adding visual interest and scale to any landscape.

There are also the boats to look out for. Amongst the modern white plastic holiday cruisers, there are many traditional vessels, from the huge barge like Norfolk wherries, to the traditional sailing cruisers and elegant polished racing yachts. Catching one of these as they pass a traditional windmill makes the perfect picture of the Norfolk Broads.

Many river trips are on offer or you can explore on your own by hiring a boat for the day.

DON'T MISS

Ranworth broad and church
St Benet's abbey
Cockshoot Broad
Thurne Dyke
Barton Broad

48. HICKLING BOAT HOUSES

The largest and bleakest of the Norfolk Broads, home to the best collection of traditional thatched boat houses.
NR12 0BT Hill Common boat houses
NR12 0YW car park charges
NR12 0BW Wildlife Trust charges

49. HORSEY DRAINAGE MILL

One of the most photographed views in Norfolk, with the windmill overlooking the boats moored below.
NR29 4EF NT car park with walk around the marsh and broad.

50. MARTHAM BROAD

Hickling's smaller sister, Martham Broad is tucked away amongst the marshes, reached by a walk along the southern bank of the River Thurne from West Somerton Staithe. There is an interesting circler walk past the broad and derelict wind pump to Martham Ferry Dyke and back across the fields.

NR29 4EB West Somerton Staithe
NR29 4RG Martham Ferry Dyke

51. THURNE DYKE

A pretty small hamlet on the River Ant, with wind pumps on either bank, still with their sails, this is a busy part of the river for boats old and new. Footpaths lead along the banks, part of the 56 mile Weavers' Way trail.

NR29 3BU free on street parking

THE BROADS

52. UPTON

This is home to a traditional boatyard. The Dyke leads to the River Thurne, with its disused wind pumps once used to drain the surrounding farmland.
The adjacent nature reserve is a hidden gem, made up of a patchwork of Broadland habitats.
NR13 6EQ nature reserve
NR13 6BL free car park

53. POTTER HEIGHAM

A Broads village full of boatyards, the arches of the medieval bridge are the most difficult to navigate on the whole Broads network.
NR29 5JQ small layby beside the bridge

52

52

THE BROADS

THE BROADS

THE BROADS

54. HOW HILL

A popular spot on the River Ant, with nice walks, typical of Broadland. A couple of windmills add to the scene.
NR29 5PG free carpark beside study centre. The path to the river is across the lawn below the house.

55. RANWORTH

A quintessential Broads village around a staithe, fringed by woodland. The church is nicknamed the "Cathedral of the Broads", and is filled with medieval paintings. The tower is open, giving a high vantage point over the Broads landscape. There is also a boardwalk path, through woodland carr and marsh to a floating visitor centre on the edge of one of the Broads. If you only visit one spot on the Broads, this should be it.
NR13 6HY free parking at staithe and church

THE BROADS

56. WOODBASTWICK

Quaint village around a small triangular green with a thatched well.
NR13 6HH

57. COCKSHOOT BROAD

Reached by a lane through the reed beds which often floods, Cockshoot Broad has been dammed off from the river to improve the water quality. The crystal clear water is home to the best of Broads wildlife, from otters to the occasional migrating osprey.
NR13 6HN parking down by river

58. WROXHAM

The capital of the Broads, home to the holiday boating industry and a bit of a tourist trap. The area around the bridge is a good place to people watch, as holidaymakers try to navigate their boats through this, the busiest part of the Broads network. Also a good place to take to the water yourself on a boat trip or by hiring a small day boat.
NR12 8RX pay and display

59. BARTON TURF

A charming collection of boatyards with a path that leads through to the River Ant. To the south is the large Barton Broad. A boardwalk leads through the reed beds to a viewing platform on the edge of the broad which is popular with sailors.
NR12 8AZ car park for staithe
NR12 8XP car park and footpath to Barton Broad

© Kelly's guides

60

60. ST BENET'S ABBEY

Built close to the junction of the rivers Bure and Ant, the ruins occupy a very isolated site at the heart of the Broads. The remains of the medieval gate house have the stump of a windmill growing out of it. This has been a popular spot for painters and photographers for the last two centuries.

NR29 5NU concrete farm track leads down to small car park

60

THE BROADS

62. ROCKLAND BROAD

A large expanse of water reached by walking along the dyke from the village, past a bird watching hide, the path continues out onto the marsh beyond.

NR14 7HP free car park

63. REEDHAM FERRY

The last vehicle ferry left in Norfolk, it is a short cut between the north and south broads. The marshland and riverside paths are a great place to capture Norfolk's Big Skies.

NR13 3HA

61. WHITLINGHAM COUNTRY PARK

On the edge of Norwich, this Broad was converted from old gravel workings and has a path all the way around. The Broad itself is not connected to the rest of the network, which makes it popular with sailors and wildlife. At the far end of the lane through the park there is another path out along the river past cottages and boatyards.

NR14 8TR pay and display

Norfolk for photographers

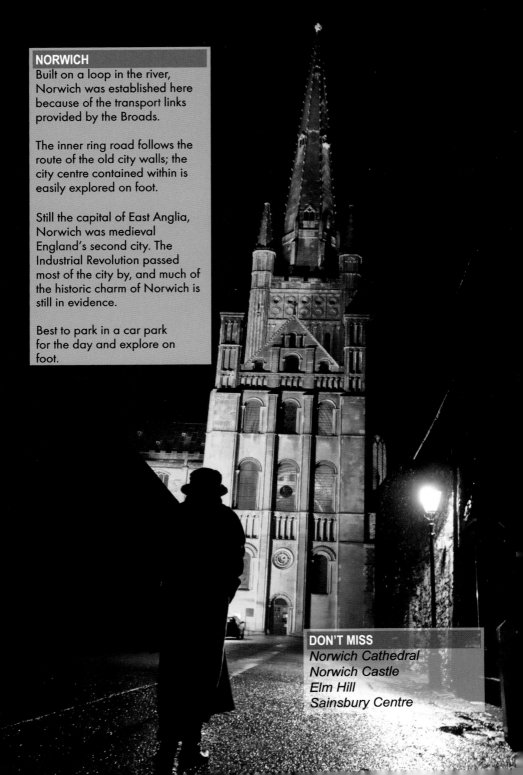

NORWICH

Built on a loop in the river, Norwich was established here because of the transport links provided by the Broads.

The inner ring road follows the route of the old city walls; the city centre contained within is easily explored on foot.

Still the capital of East Anglia, Norwich was medieval England's second city. The Industrial Revolution passed most of the city by, and much of the historic charm of Norwich is still in evidence.

Best to park in a car park for the day and explore on foot.

DON'T MISS
Norwich Cathedral
Norwich Castle
Elm Hill
Sainsbury Centre

64. NORWICH CATHEDRAL

With its tall slender spire, the cathedral is the most impressive building in the whole of Norfolk. During construction, the Normans shipped in the stone from their native France; it arrived at the water gate of Pulls Ferry. Today the yellow stone glows in the sunlight especially at dawn or dusk.

NR1 4EL pay and display on Bishopsgate at the rear of the cathedral. A gate leads into the Close.

65. THE CLOISTERS

These cloisters are the largest in the country and have their own free access from the Close. They contain fantastic and fantastical roof bosses, medieval carvings famous for biblical scenes and pagan symbols. Look up to spot Noah's Ark and the Green Men.

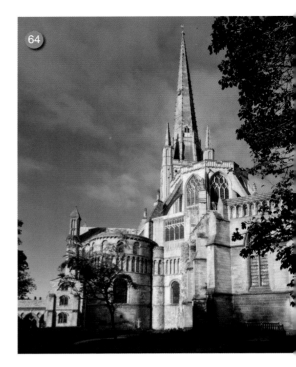

66. THE CLOSE

The extensive Cathedral Close consists of a network of streets radiating from a green. The style of the houses ranges over many eras, some with their upper stories overhanging the narrow streets. Two imposing gates divide the Close from the rest of the city.

67. ELM HILL

This is the most photographed street in Norfolk. Famously the city council wanted to knock it down in the sixties. Its preservation was a notable success for the fledging preservation movement.
NR3 1HG

68. NORWICH RIVERSIDE

The riverside path leads all the way through the city centre. From Quayside to Carrow Bridge, the path makes an interesting walk.

69. NORWICH QUAYSIDE

Once Norwich's port, this area is a recent success of the heritage industry. Although the buildings look old many are modern conversions on the site of old factories. Now the brightly coloured buildings reflect in the river.
NR3 1RQ The riverside path continues behind the law courts with an imposing Victorian former warehouse on the other bank. Pass a modern footbridge and continue to the next bend in the river.

70. COW TOWER

Like a small castle at the bend in the river, this tower once housed a chain which closed off the entrance to the port.
NR1 4AA Continue downstream and cross the river at the medieval Bishops Bridge. Turn right along the far bank.

NORWICH

71. PULLS FERRY

With the river in the foreground and cathedral behind, this is a scene on many a chocolate box. The arch once spanned the canal built up to the cathedral, used to deliver stone during construction.

NR1 1SR The path continues past the station and through a retail development with two modern swing bridges. Carrow Road marks the outer boundary of Medieval Norwich. Turn right up Carrow Hill.

© Kelly's guides

72. THE BLACK TOWER

Along the ridge can be seen
some imposing remnant of the
old city walls. From here Ber
Street leads back into the city
centre

NR1 2AJ

73. NORWICH MARKET

At the heart of Norwich is the market. Although modernised the stalls still retain their colourful charm. To one side is the Medieval Guild Hall, its intricate flint work is worth closer inspection.
NR2 1ND

74. CITY HALL

The market and much of the city centre is dominated by the Edwardian City Hall. Its scale and proportions are imposing and elegant.
NR2 1NH

© Kelly's guides

75. THE FORUM

This was a millennium project
built to replace the city library
which burnt down in 1998.
Look out for the reflections
of the church opposite in the
Forum's glass frontage.
NR2 1AW

76. NORWICH CASTLE

Two streets away from the
market is Norwich Castle. There
is a path around the mound
which offers good views
over the city. There is also a
battlements tour with even finer
views.
NR1 3JU

77. MOUSEHOLD

High heath with a vantage point looking over Norwich; a good place to photograph the cities two cathedrals and other landmarks. In the old barracks buildings is a great cafe, run as part of a rehabilitation program for prisoners from the neighbouring prison.

NR1 4HJ free car park

78. UEA

Much of the campus of the university was built in the brutalist style popular in the 1960s, much of which, in the rest of the country, has been demolished or neglected but not here. In this parkland setting, the pyramid halls of residence or Ziggurats are striking, also of architectural interest is the Sainsbury Centre, an important building from Norman Fosters early career.

There is a lovely walk around the lake, and there are many interesting shapes to be photographed amongst the architecture, walkways and spiral staircases.

NR4 7AR limited free parking on the edge of the campus or NR4 7RQ parking by roundabout and walk down through woods and past lake.

Norfolk for photographers

79. BIXLEY CHURCH

Many Norfolk churches have been in ruins for centuries. This church was destroyed by fire only a decade ago. The structure is obviously unsafe so keep your distance.
NR14 8RY up track off B1332 beware no parking on busy road

80. HANWORTH

An unusual village set amongst common land still used for graving, its bigger neighbour of Aldborough has a village cricket pitch on its green.
NR11 7HP parking around common

81. BLICKLING HALL

This huge parkland has the Jacobean hall at its centre. The imposing front elevation of the hall is flanked by two wings, the line continuing with high yew hedges. The meadow facing the front of the house is crossed by a path, with a view of the house within a wider landscape. The rear of the hall overlooks a lake. Beyond the lake, in the woods, is an imposing pyramid mausoleum, and a lodge with tower once used to watch horse racing. The estate is so extensive it's nice to explore by bike. Look out for the free parking around the edge of the estate with great walks to hall
NR11 6NF NT car park
NR11 6PU free lake car park
NR11 6PY free rear car park
NR11 6PA free tower car park

INLAND

Norfolk for photographers

SAINTS AND ANGELS

So rich is Norfolk with interesting churches, a whole guide could be written about them.

As you look across the Landscape the horizon is punctuated by church towers.

Norfolk churches are famous for their carved angels, which are used to decorate the structure of the intricate roofs and beams. They were used from the medieval period and more were added during Victorian restorations.

They vary in number, size and decoration. As they are high up in often dark roofs, they can be a challenge to photograph. But using a tripod or flash, is a good exercise if the weather turns wet outside.

DON'T MISS
Booton Angels
Cawston Angels
Wiggenhall St Mary's
Snetterton war memorial

82

82. CAWSTON ANGELS

The little town of Cawston has a big church. The plain tower rises like a monolith over the surrounding houses, but its the inside and the angels holding up the roof beams that impress the most.

NR10 4AG park outside church

83. SCOTTOW DUAL CARRIAGEWAY

This is the most bizarre entry in this guide; a single track country lane suddenly becomes a dual carriageway for no apparent reason. Not really worth a visit but fun.

INLAND

84 .LITTLE WITCHINGHAM CHURCH

This small redundant church has richly decorated walls dating from the 14th century
NR9 5PA limited parking at church

85. SWANTON MORLEY

The rivers of Norfolk are not all about the Broads, This village lies on the edge of the Wensum Valley. A path by the side of the church leads down to the river, with a typical round tower church on the far bank.
NR20 4PB parking beside church

86. CASTLE ACRE

This is one of the prettiest villages in Norfolk. It boasts a castle and a priory. What remains of the castle is its impressive earthworks, a series of high banks and ditches. The best views of the Priory are from the field between the site and the village church.

PE32 2AE free parking around village

PE32 2XB castle free

PE32 2AA priory admission charges

87. HOUGHTON HALL

A stately home still in private hands, which gives it a different atmosphere to the corporate National Trust feel of many other estates in Norfolk. The gardens are home to works of modern sculpture, and the layout of the gardens is still evolving and not locked in a specific place in time.

PE31 6UE admission charges

INLAND

INLAND

88. WALSINGHAM

This was once a major pilgrimage site. It is home to many Christian shrines. Pilgrims can still be seen carrying crosses along the country lanes as they near the end of their journey. There is a major procession through the village at Easter, with vocal demonstrations from different Christian sects.

NR22 6BP pay and display car park

89. BIRCHAM WINDMILL

A working flour mill which is open to the public. You can climb to the top and get up-close to the massive cogs and gears used to drive the mill stones.

PE31 6SJ admission charges

90. BOOTON ANGELS

A gothic folly of a church built by a rich Victorian playboy-come-vicar. The roof is held up by beautiful carved wooden angels.

NR10 4NZ parking at church

INLAND

91. WYMONDHAM ABBEY

A pleasant market town with the Market Cross and interesting abbey with twin towers.
NR18 0PH parking around abbey

92. THETFORD WARREN LODGE

Breckland is a distinctive landscape which straddles the Norfolk Suffolk border. Open sandy heathlands fringed by Scots pine. Much of the area was planted with conifers to create Thetford Forest. The ruins of Thetford Warren Lodge sit on the edge of the forest.
IP27 0AF free parking

93. OXBURGH HALL

A medieval moated great house, the walls of Oxburgh Hall rise straight out of the water. Arguably the best country house in Norfolk.
PE33 9PS NT admission charges

INLAND

© Kelly's guides

(94)

94. THETFORD PRIORY

Surrounded by the modern
town, all that remains of the
extensive priory are the flint
core of the walls, columns and
arches, weathered by centuries
to look like rows of stalagmites.
IP24 1BB parking parallel to
main road and bridge
IP24 2DP on street parking

95. DISS

On the southern edge of
Norfolk, Diss is an unspoiled
market town, set around the
edge of a pretty lake called the
Mere.
IP22 4LB pay and display car
park next to park and Mere

96. CAPTAIN MAINWARING

The exteriors for the BBC's
Dad's Army were shot in and
around Thetford. This statue
marks the fact.
IP24 3AD on street parking

97. THETFORD CASTLE

In a park on the edge of the
town is the earthwork remains of
a Motte and Bailey castle, The
huge Motte is one of the largest
historical manmade mound in
the country.
IP24 2DP on street parking

98. HEYDON

Quiet village and estate. No car park or gift shop, just an unspoilt village with pub, bakery and tea rooms. Through the park gates sits the house amongst trees and parkland.
NR11 6AD parking in village

99. SWAFFHAM WIND TURBINE

So often seen as a blot on the landscape the turbine at the eco centre in Swaffham is unique in having a viewing platform at the top.
PE37 7HT admission charges apply

98

99

100. SNETTERTON MEMORIAL

The American Air Force had 18 airfields across Norfolk during the Second World War. The county is dotted with memorials, commemorating the huge loss of life amongst the air crews. This memorial is the most modern and striking; it depicts a B17 climbing into the sky.

NR16 2JU beside entrance to Snetteron circuit park by the memorial if there is not a event on

EQUIPMENT

Over recent years the development in camera technology has been huge.

The resolution of smart phone cameras is now equal to that of very expensive professional cameras from a few years ago.

There is a saying in photography, "the best camera is the one you have with you".

Expensive camera, lens and a tripod are all very nice, but a smart phone is all you need and capable of much more than just selfies.

TECHNIQUE

The automatic settings on cameras cope very well with most situations. The camera has to guess what it is, in the picture, you are interested in. For example: Is it the tree, the building, or the mountain behind that's important. The camera then adjusts the settings accordingly.

When you look at your picture, check that it's the main subject within the frame that looks correct. Check that it looks in focus and is not too light or dark. Adjust the settings to get the results you're looking for.

COMPOSITION

Good composition is what makes any photograph stand out. Look for something in the foreground, like wild flowers in a field or a sandcastle on a beach to add interest and depth. Look for gaps in hedges and gates in walls, to use as a natural frame.

Diagonal lines in a picture formed by a path or hedge can be used to point the viewer to the main element in the composition.

TECHNIQUE

Weather can be everything to a good landscape. Don't restrict yourself to bright summer days. Sunshine and showers can be dramatic as the sun breaks through the clouds. Even a forecast of mist shouldn't stop you going out with your camera. Trees and buildings can look very moody set against a misty background.

A seascape can change depending on the state of the tide. It's worth checking tide tables.

The time around dawn and dusk is known by photographers as the golden hour. The qualities of the light can be literally golden. Also the oblique angle of the sun light casts great shadows.

TECHNIQUE

Little Witchingham Church 92

USEFUL WEBSITES

www.norfolk-broads-review.co.uk
Information about many of the broads

www.enjoythebroads.com
Broads National Park

www.norfolkwildlifetrust.org.uk
Nature reserves across Norfolk

www.visitnorfolk.co.uk
Tourist information

www.visitchurches.org.uk
Organisation which looks after many
interesting redundant churches

www.norfolkchurches.co.uk
Guide to Norfolk's churches

www.beansboattrips.co.uk
Blakeney boat trips

www.bing.com/mapspreview
Online maps with Ordnance Survey

Stephen Kelly

Born in the Black Country, photographer Stephen Kelly has lived in Norfolk for thirty years. His work has taken him around the world from covering wars in the Balkans and Middle East to motorsport in the Far East and South America.

kellysguides@gmail.com